I CAME WHILE YOU WERE SLEEPING

Finley & Johnson

P.31 WIVES CLUB

Published by: Manifested Truth Publishing

www.p31wivesclub.com

ISBN: 978-1-7357567-6-9

Printed in the United States of America

TABLE OF CONTENTS

DEDICATION

We dedicate this book to every woman that understands and embodies what it takes to be a Proverbs 31 wife. Know that God sees all, knows all, and will cause you to recover all. Stand firmly in the power, faith, & assurance that God is for you and your marriage! He will wipe every tear, heal every place of hurt, mend every broken piece, as well as resurrect and restore even the marriage or situation that seems unfixable.

Your enemies will not prosper over nor against you. The Lord will send his swift and mighty judgement to bring you justice for offenses done against you. Trust in the Lord, submit to his transformation, be healed, be restored, be delivered, forgive and live free.

GENESIS 2:21

“And the Lord God caused a deep sleep to fall upon Adam, and he slept...”

1. Created for Paradise

Genesis 2:7-8 "And the LORD God formed man of the dust of the ground and breathed into his nostrils the breath of life; and man became a living soul. And the LORD God planted a garden eastward in Eden; and there he put the man whom he had formed." (**KJV**)

I Genesis 2: 7-21 tells us exactly who Adam was, how he came to be, and what God's design, thoughts, and plans were concerning his human creation. Verse seven tells us that Adam was **formed** (*organized in a way characteristic of living matter*) of the dust of the ground and ***God breathed*** into man's nostrils; ***the breath of life***; and man ***became a living soul***. The first revelation we must understand is that a man can be driven, handsome, financially successful, nice, and many other good things, but until he accepts Christ into his life, he will not be a "living soul". God created Adam who represents every man on the earth today.

Man was created with a specific purpose in mind, but if today's man doesn't understand their need to know God their creator, it will be impossible for them to understand their roles in relationships, especially marriage as well as their authority and role in the earth as God's son and heir to His throne.

Verses eight through fourteen speak in detail about the garden God planted as well as the trees and rivers he created to sustain the life of both man, and the garden He created for man. We know that this garden was created to inhabit/house man because verse eight declares, "***And the Lord God planted a garden eastward***

in Eden; and there he put the man whom he formed." I began to imagine how this garden looked, what the weather may have felt like, and even what scent would fill my nose if I were standing directly where God placed man and I realized that God didn't just make man to run wild or wander aimlessly throughout the earth. He created a paradise for man to dwell in. It is for this very reason that men in today's society can seem lost or unaware when God is not the center of their lives, influencing their desires, thought patterns, and decision making. Everyone wants to live in a paradise. Most men want to have an amazing woman by their side, but how can he truly take care of all that he has been giving responsibility for, how can he recognize what paradise is supposed to look like for him, and how will he know how to choose that woman who is going to benefit and compliment his life and purpose without that personal relationship with Christ?

The definition of the word paradise according to Merriam Webster's Dictionary is: "a very beautiful, pleasant, or peaceful place that seems to be perfect." It's not until a man understands and embraces God's original plan for his life that he is capable of maintaining, appreciating, and enjoying the paradise God created just for him.

P We were created to live in our beautiful paradise, this is why we must come to a place of obedience and understanding of our paradise. When reading these scriptures, you see just how GOD created such a beautiful place for Adam long before Eve was even brought onto the scene. This causes me to believe that even today GOD has given men the keys to their family's paradise. The example that immediately comes to my mind is, Abraham and Sarah. He was an obedient and righteous man who was able to lead his wife and family into a new land of prosperity and abundance. They lived in that original type of paradise that God had always intended.

Now ask yourself, what happens when that man is sleeping in his garden? Well, we know the enemy comes to steal, kill & destroy right? In today's scenario, what happens if the man is sleep in the home, but the wife is awake, praying, preparing, and gleaning from God while he's asleep? When that woman's husband does awake, he will come into a garden that the enemy was not able to discombobulate, because his help mate wasn't asleep. Men, it's important to choose a wife who can cover you while God is working on you, and when you find that kind of woman and make her your wife, appreciate who she is and who she's been called to be to you, because while you were asleep, she was being equipped.

2. Handcrafted

P One day over 5 years ago while I was up praying, I mean I was in some serious warfare prayer. The Lord had me to stop and look at my husband while he was asleep. I asked God how he could sleep while I was up praying for his family. God then reminded me that while my husband is sleeping, things are taking place within him. Yes, he left me up alone to pray for our family but while he's asleep God was busy creating within me all that I would need to become the woman my husband desires to be with.

I can imagine God's voice speaking to me in that moment saying, "I even put Adam to sleep while I made Eve because it would be things that Adam and many husbands to come would do today that could stop the destiny on their wife's life. So let him sleep, while I keep working on you."

God's words to my spirit comforted me as I heard, "when the appropriate timing comes, he (your husband) will rise up and see that just like I handcrafted Eve for Adam, I also handcrafted Patrice for Maurice!" When GOD gave me that revelation I was confused. I thought I was already handcrafted well for my husband; little did I know I was only touching the surface while he was still asleep.

God will handcraft a woman to fit for a man's desires. If we remain patient with the process, it can create something beautiful in the end. This process reminds me of a caterpillar's metamorphous of turning into a butterfly; the way it's uniquely crafted and created while safely tucked away in its cocoon. When it exits from that state it emerges as one of the God's most beautiful creations.

Genesis 2:21, *"And the Lord God caused a deep sleep to fall upon Adam, and he slept: and he took one of his ribs and closed up the flesh instead thereof; 22 and the rib, which the Lord God had taken from man, made he a woman, and brought her unto the man." (***KJV***)*

The Lord caused a deep sleep to fall upon Adam. This means that Adam's sleep was intentional. I imagine he was put to sleep for two main reasons: first to protect Adam from feeling the pain of the surgery. This leads me to believe that when the time comes for a man to receive his spouse, it should be painless. It should be painless because for both man and woman, single life should be a blissful, insightful, and fulfilling preparation time period. Before God deemed it time for Adam's help meet, Adam had already been busy hearing, obeying, and carrying God's instructions for him in his daily life. Adam already had an intimate relationship with God (as the bible says they walked together in the cool of the day).

Adam had been obedient, faithful, and diligent and God looked upon him and recognized that the beast and fowl upon the earth had a mate, but Adam did not. For men, a wife should only be sought out when he reaches the place within his life where he is being busy, obedient to God fulfilling his destiny, and has a solid, intimate relationship with God and he is now ready to have a "help meet" to fulfill his creation role as husband, father, priest, and protector. This means he must not just be ready and capable to handle the responsibility, but he must welcome it and desire to have a partner to do life with.

The second reason I imagine from the scriptures text is, that God knew what to do and how to bring about the mate that would be compatible with Adam so there was no need for him to be awake to see God work his magic. I can speak from experience and say that as human beings, we can't handle everything. We will always want to be in control of our own lives. We will always want to know as much as we can. We don't like leaning and depending on others for things we need. If we can make or do something ourselves, we will so that we don't have to pay someone else to do it for us. There are so many times where we as human beings get in God's way. We don't mean to do it. We certainly don't think that God needs our expertise and assistance, but our nature compels us to put our hands in it some way somehow.

When God is ready to bless you with your spouse, your partner, and teammate for life: He doesn't need your help doing it, He just needs your obedience to receive it, take care of it, appreciate it, and enjoy it. Although I do not believe there is this one perfect soul mate for every person. I do believe that God will guide you and give you wisdom to choose the person that will compliment, help, and be a partner in your life and godly purpose here on this earth. In this regard there is a woman that has been handcrafted through God's preparation to be your wife.

3. The Subtle Intruder

P "Did God say, You must not eat fruit from any tree of the garden?" This is what satan asked Eve in the garden. As I'm writing this while sitting in my actual garden, with my husband fast asleep. I realize just how divine this is. God put my entire house to sleep just so I would have the peace and quiet needed to put on these pages what God has instilled within my heart, mind, and spirit. This chapter was divinely orchestrated for me to write on purpose, today!

This morning when I arose, I had an opportunity to set our household atmosphere right. I began with worship to combat the spirit of heaviness. After worship I began to war through prayer, for I have learned how to keep the cunning enemy out of our home, mind, and bed. I have learned what is necessary to stop allowing him access. This all took place within our garden. Our garden has become a sacred place where I have given God complete access.

When the husband is asleep spiritually in the home, he gives the woman the right and the authority as his wife to help him create. A good wife will not do anything that can harm her garden (home/dwelling place) while her husband is asleep. The kinds of things a spouse can do to harm their garden includes but is not limited to, gossiping, lusting, drinking, smoking, cursing him and the children, and much more. Every home as their own specific targets sent to destroy the home. I'm just sharing common ways/methods the enemy will use to steal, kill, and destroy.

It's valuable to have one or both spouses consistently/daily praying for their spouse, marriage, and family because when the enemy catches both spouses asleep, there is an open door for the enemy to bring chaos into your garden and ruin all the work God has had you building there. I can remember when my husband and I both fell asleep in our garden and boy did the enemy come in our home and wreck it, all while we were sleeping.

I want to warn you today that you're dealing with a subtle intruder. All it takes is one open door or one gateway for the enemy to get in. Some people don't realize it until it's too far gone, and they don't see any hope of fighting.

Others see the enemy but aren't equipped to fight him because their relationship with God is lacking, non-existent, or has waxed cold, which leaves them powerless against the enemy's devices. I want to speak to the spirit of every wife today when I say, "Eve, hold the garden down if that's where GOD has positioned you to be because that will cause your household to be blessed.

Unfortunately, there may come a time when your husband will choose to roam from the garden, he's supposed to take care of (you, your children, and your home) but even in those moments you cannot allow his absence to distract you from going to war against the enemy because if you do, you will give entry into your home to the intruder and he will bring disaster not only for today but for generations to come, sis!! Your emotions and logic will have you angry at your husband for falling asleep on the job, but don't you go to sleep because he is, somebody must stay woke, alert, and diligent in the fight.

Genesis 3:1 "*Now the serpent was more subtle than any beast of the field which the Lord God had made. And he said unto the woman, Yea, hath God said, Ye shall not eat of every tree of the garden*?" (**KJV**)

I absolutely love how our God never leaves you in the dark about the adversary you're facing. Those of us who read the scriptures today to follow the guidance and instructions of God can receive valuable information as we walk out our Christ-like journey in this earth. Marriage is not just a piece of paper you get to validate your love. Marriage is a God orchestrated relational bond, and he loves us and that bond so much that he declares in ***Mark 10:9 "What therefore God hath joined together, let not man put asunder***" (KJV)

It's because God loves His people and the covenant of marriage that he warns us of the dangerous enemy that has come to separate/divide the covenant he ordained, and that you and your spouse chose to enter. This particular scripture text lets us know that the serpent is the most subtle: meaning slick, sneaky, conniving, cunning/wise of all the beast of the field. We see this to be true based on the facts that the serpent's conversation in the garden that day with Eve led to the separation of her, Adam, and God's three-fold cord relationship. This conversation led to multiple curses being introduced to a paradise life in a paradise world that had been created by God especially for mankind. It also led to the introduction of a new way of living that was harder and full of turmoil. I say all of this to mimic to you Adam & Eve's example to us as spouses that the enemy, which is satan, that old serpent is after your covenant marriage.

When we don't understand who the enemy is within our marriage, how to defeat him, and how to recognize when he shows up on the scene; we put our marriage covenant and all the work we have done to build and maintain godly order within our lives and home in jeopardy. When battling godly marriages/spouses the enemy doesn't show up loud and bold, he sneaks his way into the cracks to minimize chances of defeat. That is the reason the enemy must first divide the husband and wife before he can destroy the marriage altogether, which is his ultimate target.

Too often we don't recognize the enemy at work until situations have gone too far. When the spouse cheats, moves out, raises their hands to assault their spouse, etc. it's the end result of all the little things the enemy has been doing for weeks, months, and maybe years to create a separation/drift/or break within your covenant marriage. The bonds of marriage are so strong that God declares that they are no longer two but one flesh. Marriage God's way bonds a husband

and wife to one another so deeply that God no longer sees two fleshly beings but one. They share the joys and sadness of life, the dreams and doubts, the struggles, and successes. What happens to one of them, happens to the other as well.

The enemy may have already done damage to your marriage with his subtle/evasive maneuvering which has resulted in strain, anxiety, and uneasiness within your home. It may have resulted in separation and maybe even divorce, but I promise you that it is never too late to repent to God for what you've done or for not standing in the gap for your marriage and spouse. It's not too late to give yourself, your spouse, marriage, and family to God to repair and restore. The process may not be quick or easy, but God will show up if you stay diligent and faithful to Him and your covenant.

Remember that the enemy comes to steal, kill, and to destroy. Your marriage bond is a threat to the enemy because it mirrors God's love for his people, His kingdom order in the earth, and it embodies the example of all he teaches us to follow in his word. The more marriages the enemy destroys and keeps apart; the more mankind begins to create their own way of doing life that's contrary to God's principles and examples. The enemy is sneaky, so be diligent in prayer, in your relationship with God as well as in your love, faithfulness, and dedication to your spouse and family and watch God bring you through every trial you face victorious.

4. The Bite Together

Genesis 3:6-7 "*And when the woman saw that the tree was good for food, and that it was pleasant to the eyes, and a tree to be desired to make one wise, she took of the fruit thereof, and did eat, and gave also unto her husband with her; and he did eat. And the eyes of them both were opened, and they knew that they were naked; and they sewed fig leaves together and made themselves aprons.*" **(KJV)**

Before I dive into the meat of my thoughts concerning this chapter's content, I believe it's extremely important that we go to the scriptures first. At the end of the previous chapter, we see that satan has manipulated the words of God by telling Eve that God said she couldn't eat of any tree of the garden, when in fact God told Adam that they could eat of all the trees except the Tree of Knowledge of Good and Evil. It's just like the enemy to try to distort God's word. Clearly Eve knew what God really said because she immediately corrects the serpent, but he puts yet another doubt in her mind by telling her, "you will not surely die. The serpent goes on to outline three things that is going to happen when she eats of the forbidden fruit: 1. Her eyes will be opened 2. She and Adam would be as gods and 3. They will know both good and evil.

I want you to pay close attention because God's word is a guide to us today. The truth of the matter is the enemy isn't using new tactics. His devices and strategies to destroy marriages and families is the same. He must first convince you to go against God's instructions. The enemy gets very smart and slick with his approach but if you pay close attention, the root of the trap is still the same. He tries to get you in a state of confusion by speaking the opposite of what God speaks to you. This is especially important for husbands and wives to observe because most infidelity started long before the physical act occurred.

Every marriage faces challenges and goes through cycles where love and attraction dwindle and aren't as strong as it once was. That is supposed to be a clue for the spouses to find their way back to one another through prayer, God's instructions, and application and effort. However, what often happens is they allow the issues, differences, indifferent feelings to put more distance between them, causing an emotional separation.

The emotional separation is dangerous because now the spouse is open to the suggestions and voice of the enemy that often times comes as a friend/associate of the opposite sex. Before they know it, they feel they can trust this new person more than their spouse, and they somehow become so convinced that this friend/associate sees the real them and thinks better of them than their spouse does. This is of course not true, but it's the narrative the enemy is now feeding the person who may be bored, tired of trying and fighting, or feels like they're not getting what they deserve or being treated as well as they should.

Almost 100% of the time the spouse doesn't look at their own actions, instead they hold on to the voice of the enemy as it speaks through the distracting forces. They cling to the distracting voices because it's better than having to take accountability for their actions or lack thereof. And just like that, you're in a mental space where you're ready to sacrifice your family, the life you've built, and the love you were once so excited to have in that spouse.

The greatest danger is that in those moments you also turn your back on the God who saved and redeemed your life, because His instructions to you would be to repent to Him, make things right with your spouse, and build a better union together. Every spouse that ever truly loved God yet chose to turn their backs on their marriage has heard God speak loudly to his/her spirit not to do it or to go back home, but you ignored His voice in order to do what you wanted to do.

This is exactly what happened with Eve. She knew the truth of what God said, but because she chose to continue to conversate and entertain the serpent. Doing what she wanted to do, brought confusion to her mind and then she did the worse thing ever, she relied upon her eyes, thoughts, and perceptions to make a life changing decision. You see this when the scripture says, "***when the woman saw that the tree was good for food and pleasant to the eyes, and a tree to be desired to make one wise, she took the fruit and did eat, and gave also unto her husband with her and he did eat***."

When it comes to Adam's part in this, it's always been a strong topic of debate. Some people felt like she had the conversation with the serpent, ate the fruit, and then went and persuaded Adam to eat as well. However, if you study the scripture text it tells you that she gave to her husband Adam **WITH** her, and he did eat! This means that Adam was right there as the serpent and Eve were having the dialogue back and forth. This gives me insight into today's issues between husband and wife as well.

Adam's role in the sin within the garden is no different from the issues that marriages face when the husband doesn't fully embrace and take accountability of his role as the head of the home and family. If Adam had been operating in his headship, he would have stopped that conversation before it really even got started. He allowed the open space for the enemy to address Eve and he allowed her to step into a place of authority to allow her to speak for them both when he was the one that God actually gave the rules and commandments of the garden to.

When men sit down on their jobs, they lose the respect of the women their supposed to be leading. When a husband takes a back seat on the duties God gave directly to him, he pushes his wife out of her position and comfortability to have to take his place as "the head", but then he will feel disrespected and destroyed by her because he doesn't recognize that he has inadvertently switched their roles. This is a major problem in many marriages and homes today. It's very important to study, understand, discuss, and agree on the specific duties and roles each spouse is expected to be responsible for within the marriage and family unit before marriage is embarked upon.

Another concept or idea I see visible through the scripture text is that Adam remembered what God said would happen if they did not obey his instructions concerning the tree. He said they would surely die, and Adam knew that Eve would be put out of the garden for her disobedience. I truly believe that Adam didn't want to be separated from his wife. If she had to go, so did he. Adam was the very first "ride or die" spouse/companion!

P It is my opinion that today many men in marriages are inviting their godly wives to sin with them, knowing what will happen if they both disobey GOD. Now, it's one thing for one spouse to be asleep but when you have two lost souls eating the fruits of death together, then everybody suffers. Adam chose to listen to his wife and eat with her, and surely did they die, not only did they die, but they destroyed generations.

There are generations even unto this day that are still crawling from their pit of the bite together. It's important in marriages for both spouses to be on one accord in obedience to God, but at the very minimum one spouse at least needs to be obedient to GOD. A lot of times it will be the woman that is the one standing in obedience. You may be asking why the woman, when the man is ordained to be the head. The answer is simple, it's because the man is too busy sleeping and allowing the enemy to toil with his mind, Awe but that praying wife can see well and she has the ability to bind and loose that bondage off of her husband because she is receiving the blessings of the Lord and if she stays consistent, obedient, and sincere: her prayers will not go unanswered. Imagine how differently the garden experience would've been if only Eve took a stand and/or Adam stood in his authority as protector and leader.

I close this chapter with a warning for every wife dealing with a sleeping husband; you cannot force him wake up (although it is in our nature to attempt to encourage the change we see is needed), so you will have to allow him to sleep sis. Don't bite that apple with him. I know it looks good and I know it sounds good, trust me I understand. It might even taste good (as the wrong thing often feels good) but it isn't worth the destruction that's going to come from that sin against GOD"

5. The Fear, the Lies, & the Shame

P Has your marriage ever encountered the fear and uncertainty of what has been done in the relationship through the years? As you look back can you be honest enough to say that at some point in the marriage you were sleeping right along with your husband (blind/unaware), well that's my story too. I finally woke up, but when I did I found my husband was still asleep. I realized what we had done in that sleep state had impacted both our individual lives as well as our family and marriage.

I had to carry the fear of the consequences that would fall upon us for disobeying GOD with my husband and not allowing our home to be set up the way GOD intended for it to be. I know now that it was all a part of the set up for disaster and I would now have to deal with the fear, lies, and shame of what came from my home being out of order.

I often wondered if I would ever wake up from the nightmare I helped create out of ignorant disobedience. What would I do if my spouse never woke up from his slumber? What did God want me to do about our children? My spouse was still stuck partying and yet here I was choosing to come out of the limelight without him. We had both hidden ourselves until in the world's way of living until I came to the place of understanding and surrender. I told GOD that I wasn't going to hide anymore. I asked God to fix this garden and I didn't care what it would take nor what I would lose. Even our "Yes" to God will cost us something.

We must give God time in the marriage to uncover, the fear lies and shame, it takes dedication and prayer. To the wives that refused to give up and go hide in the world, I encourage you to keep praying to God for wisdom, strength, and transformation within because it's the only way you'll be able to help your husband tend to the garden God has given them command over.

Genesis 3:8-10 *"And they heard the voice of the LORD God walking in the garden in the cool of the day: and Adam and his wife hid themselves from the presence of the LORD God amongst the trees of the garden. And the LORD God called unto Adam, and said unto him, Where art thou? And he said, I heard thy voice in the garden, and I was afraid, because I was naked; and I hid myself."* ***(KJV)***

This scripture text shows us the 3 stages Adam & Eve went through once God confronted them about what they had done. It's simple enough for me to understand that these 3 stages are our natural human responses when we have made mistakes or bad choices and now in need of taking responsibility for it. Most people don't like to nor even understand how to truly take accountability for their actions.

The first stage they encountered was **FEAR**. When they heard God's voice in the cool of the day, they "hid" themselves from his "presence". Now this is super deep and extremely important especially for spouses to understand. After a spouse (or both) have wronged one another within the covenant of marriage it can seem like the end for both spouses. The offender may experience extreme guilt and condemnation which makes it too painful for them to even have to face their spouse whom they have wronged. Initially they will feel an extreme level of "it'll never be the same" feelings and thoughts.

In this moment the enemy capitalizes on the guilt by telling them that they will never be able to fix it, or they've done something so bad that their spouse will never forgive them nor love and see them the same. Once the guilty spouse buys into this thought they check out mentally, emotionally, and often times even physically by leaving the home and abandoning their spouse and family.

The spouse who has endured the offense also feels like it's over because they often are faced with feelings of being inadequate, unloved, deceived, or discarded. The spouse may begin to pick themselves apart looking for a reason why the spouse they loved, cherished, and made an unbreakable vow with would throw their years of a shared life together for. Both spouses are under spiritual attack in their minds which brings confusion and uncertainty.

When an offense or violation against the marriage occurs, this is the time to not make any sudden nor emotional moves. This is the time that spouses should take some time apart (not separation) to seek God's face, receive godly counsel, and bring their emotions to a place of calmness so that effective communication can occur between them to address the issue at hand and discuss a pathway to healing, forgiveness, and restoration of trust and love to ensure the marriage survives the current storm.

However, just like with Adam and Eve, most spouses fail to respond this way because they allow the fear of what will happen because of their actions to cause them to react impulsively, carrying out the first reactive idea that comes to mind which is either to hide or run. In many cases the spouse will both hide and run.

The second phase they embarked upon was **THE LIE.** God asked Adam where he was, and Adam didn't say I'm right here hiding from you because I messed up. He said that God's voice made him fearful because of his nakedness and that's why he hid, but that wasn't the whole truth. Adam hid because he ate what God told him not to eat. Realizing his nakedness was a byproduct of the sin of disobedience he performed in the garden.

This same spirit of lying can be found in the circumstances and accounts given of every broken marriage that has caused the separation or divorce between spouses. In the garden it was not just the lie, but it was also the lack of accountability that was taken for each spouse's part in the sin. When a spouse doesn't immediately go into a spirit of repentance to God for violating the marriage covenant as well as the hurt and damage their actions caused upon their spouse and family, they begin to spiral down a path to both hide from what they did and run from the responsibility of making things right.

This spiral of behavior choices will lead them to a place of trying to justify their wrong behavior. Many will tell lies or over exaggerate wrong behavior of their spouses to make them feel like what they have done was either not as bad as what the spouse had been doing to them already, or that the spouses behavior justified their offense. This is where many spouses who have violated the marriage covenant will turn themselves into victims.

The lies they now believe will be the lies they tell others because after all, no one could blame you for cheating if your spouse never wanted to have sex with you, treated you mean, or wasn't appreciative of all your efforts to financially provide for them, right? No one is gonna make you feel bad for leaving the spouse who was controlling, disrespectful, and never believed in you right?

The 3rd and last phase is **SHAME**. Adam and Eve's choices in the garden left the spirit of shame sitting upon them. They hid from God whom they had freely and excitedly communed with every day in the cool of the day before that moment. They also became ashamed of their nakedness (which was their natural state of existence). They had always been naked because it's the way God created them, and their environment was conducive to their naked state of being because it was made as their dwelling place.

I also believe that they felt ashamed for being tricked by the serpent to give up the life in their paradise God created them to have and experience. Spouses who violate the marriage covenant also experience shame. However, they almost always experience the shame at a much later time when they have already left the spouse for the other person (the bible calls her the strange woman but can be the strange man too). It can be long after the spouse abandons their family to shed themselves of the pressure and responsibility of being a husband/wife or father/mother, in exchange for a life where they can do whatever they want to do. Sometimes it's after they've gotten into a new relationship or even divorced the spouse and married again.

The feeling of shame is delayed because accountability has never been truly accepted or acknowledged by them for what they've done wrong. The truth is, no matter how far or how long a spouse runs from taking accountability. No matter how many other relationships they try to hide in, God will one day bring them to their knees; for every knee must bow and every tongue must confess that He is Lord. This means that you will have to come to a place of remorse, take accountability, repent to God, make a mends to those you've wronged, and submit to God to transform your life before you can ever receive a life of true happiness, love, or new relational success.

6. The Blame Game

Genesis 3: 11-13 "And he said, Who told thee that thou wast naked? Hast thou eaten of the tree, whereof I commanded thee that thou shouldest not eat? And the man said, The woman whom thou gavest to be with me, she gave me of the tree, and I did eat. And the LORD God said unto the woman, What is this that thou hast done? And the woman said, The serpent beguiled me, and I did eat." **(KJV)**

J God is very direct with Adam when He asks him who told him that he was naked. He went on to ask him if he's eaten from the tree that He told him not to eat from. This was his opportunity to accept responsibility for what he had done, repent and allow God to forgive him and show him how to proceed forward. Adam didn't take this chance he instead does something that will continue to be perpetuated among all parties involved. He begins the infamous "blame game"!

The sad truth is that every spouse has the same opportunity that Adam & Eve had in this very moment with God in the garden. Whatever offense or error you've done against your spouse, marriage, and ultimately God (because he ordained the covenant of marriage) is never too far, too bad, or too heavy for God. God loves us all and above that God loves and honors the relational connection of the marriage/family because it's the institute he established to be an example of His love, dedication, protection, and provision for us as His people.

God is eager to forgive our sins and offenses. He is willing to forget them and show us how to repair the damage our hands have done. He's especially excited, willing, and ready to restore the love, joy, peace, and purpose of your marriage. The truth is that human beings have feelings and emotions that can be easily damaged, but God can show you how to repair what's broken if you can submit yourself to God (pride, guilt, anger, hurt, devastation, and all) to Him to heal, deliver, and teach you a better way. Instead, spouses continue in their pride, anger, revenge, trauma, and dysfunction not realizing or being so desensitized to the pain and anguish they're causing their spouse and children by not only committing the offense, but by being dismissive and thoughtless regarding their pain & devastation. The spouse then tries to "move on" with their life as if nothing has happened.

The so-called process of moving on is already doomed from the start because of how the spouse has attempted to do so. The spouse doesn't even address the lost that they too have taken by losing their love, partner, God, and family. The chose to shove their feelings in a locked space in their mind and heart with the strongest lock they can find. They pretend to be, even try to be happy in this new existence outside of the spouse, family, and God they feel they no longer need. Ironically some wayward spouses are able to experience moments of happiness, companionship, false love that feels very real to them, and even some level of success (SOME). However, it's never real. It's a life of illusions, deception, rebellion, emptiness, and silent chaos.

Adam blames Eve for his failure. Eve blames the serpent for her failure, but God never asks the serpent about his actions. He doesn't ask the serpent because he understands exactly who he is. He knows that the enemy comes to steal, kill, and to destroy everything that God created and purposed for His people. You may be blaming your marriages issues on your spouse's actions and choices, you may be blaming yourself, and you may even be giving credit to the enemy, but the truth is… it doesn't matter who's fault it is that marital failure has occurred. What matters is the path you chose to take after the failure to get back in alignment with God. It matters how you submit to God in order to fix what you've broken with Godly instruction, hard work, love, and determination.

It matters how you submit your emotions, pain, hurt, and trauma to God asking Him to heal you, make you whole, as well as help to love, forgive, and rebuild the marriage with your spouse; understanding it will be an uphill battle but one you will win if you faint not. Every marriage will encounter storms, some may even knock you way off course to the point you feel you'll never get back on the right path. However, only the marriages where both spouses refuse to quit, stop trying, stop believing God, and stop searching for healing, help, and guidance will make it out of the storms to enjoy more peace, love, joy, happiness, abundance, and success than they had even before they went into the storm.

P We have been put in situations in our marriages where we point the fingers just like Adam and Eve, but if we change things up by not blaming each other for things that sometimes we had no control over and put the focus back on the reasons why we choose the hurt, pain, and blame we'd finally be ready to move forward to the next place of development.

Wives, we must put our husbands in God hands and remember that the blame goes only to the enemy who came to bring division into our homes. I believe it's time to take the blame off of our husbands, attack the enemy we see at the root of the issues and failures so that we can show our husbands respect, love, and compassion regardless of the actions the enemy tries to get us to focus on.

Instead of continuing to keep blaming your spouse for their past offenses, pray to God for the healing and power you will need to sincerely offer them forgiveness. The inability to forgive offenses within marriage is one of the top reasons why so many marriages have and are experiencing the curse of divorce. After being married for 16 years I can tell you that's it's important to really release your husband/wife from all the things they have done to you. It is equally important for you to seek forgiveness for what you've done to them as well as it is to forgive yourself for all the times you fell short.

Forgiveness across the board is crucial in order for any marriage to survive and eventually excel. A husband/wife that cannot forgive themselves will suffer the burden of condemnation.

Condemnation will never allow you to see the progress your spouse is making to forgive you and learn to love & trust you again. It will also affect tour mood and character because you will constantly be distracted with thoughts of what you've done. You will stay stuck and not be willing to grow or move productively in your future purposed for you by God because you'll reject everything that's good because the condemnation has tricked you into thinking you don't deserve anything good. True forgiveness (of self and your spouse) allows God to step in and deal with you and your husband/wife equally to bring out a better you, thereby creating a stronger, healthier, and happier marriage bond.

7. The Sentencing

P There are consequences when a man isn't awake enough in the spirit to make sure his marriage is at its best. This leaves the woman in a position where she must now become responsible to cover what the husband is lacking. While some women can rise to the occasion, some women are not equipped enough to step in not even briefly. This shouldn't be frowned upon nor laughed at because the truth is that it's just not her job to do so because God ordained the man to be the head.

With the 1st marriage of Adam and Eve we learned that if it's not our goal to align our marriages to look like the image GOD created it to be, then we will have experiences similar to what Adam and Eve experienced in the garden. Our sins against God and our spouses will not ever go unpunished, especially if we don't repent from a sincere place.

I don't know about you, but it's been hard knowing that we were kicked out of the garden (just as Adam and Eve were). So many homes are bearing the resemblance of banishment from the life they should have and could be living within their marriage and family. What does a life kicked out of the garden look like you may ask. It's when God has positioned the woman to take the lead because the husband is out of covenant with God and his wife. It's when that shift in headship produces jealousy and envy because now God is blessing the wife and using her instead of the husband because of her availability and willingness to please him despite the state of the husband and marriage.

When this imbalance in the home happens, many men become upset with their wife. They may even begin to attack her with implications and accusations that she is purposely trying to override his authority or that she's somehow trying to emasculate (stripping him of his manhood) or embarrassing him.

However, the man must understand that being out of place with GOD is just a horrible place to be in, it doesn't matter how much money, fame, or accomplishments a man has its disgraceful to him to be kicked out his rightful position of authority within his family and the earth. God using his wife instead of him will bring turmoil into the house.

A good wife is well aware of this too, but she cannot surrender the home defenseless to the enemy that has come to devour the family. She will rely on God's strength and grace to assist her, but the whole time she's praying for her husband to get back in his place. No wife wants her husband to not lead, love, protect, and provide for her, but until the husband awakes from his place of slumber the home will remain imbalanced and he will continue to grow in adversity against the help meet God has placed in his life.

The sentencing will come in a marriage that's out of order. Remember that God gives us a free will to choose our spouses and sometimes with our choices comes undesirable consequences. Sometimes with our choice comes generational curses. The majority of the time these consequences come from both sides (husband & wife), it's just sometimes the wife is willing to fight spiritually more than the husband to break those curses or learned behaviors operating in the marriage. If the husband/wife is still sleeping that means they're still dealing with the consequences of his/her father's house because he/she has chosen not to be obedient to "Abba", who has the keys to the kingdom which is man's access to get back to the "Tree of life".

Genesis 3:14-17 "*And the LORD God said unto the serpent, Because thou hast done this, thou art cursed above all cattle, and above every beast of the field; upon thy belly shalt thou go, and dust shalt thou eat all the days of thy life: And I will put enmity between thee and the woman, and between thy seed and her seed; it shall bruise thy head, and thou shalt bruise his heel. Unto the woman he said, I will greatly multiply thy sorrow and thy conception; in sorrow thou shalt bring forth children; and thy desire shall be to thy husband, and he shall rule over thee. And unto Adam he said, Because thou hast hearkened unto the voice of thy wife, and hast eaten of the tree, of which I commanded thee, saying, Thou shalt not eat of it: cursed is the ground for thy sake; in sorrow shalt thou eat of it all the days of thy life*" **(KJV)**

I Wives and husbands, we've now come to the part of Adam & Eve's story that so many read quickly over with little to no thought about how their punishment back then affects us even today. There were three parties involved in this sin/failure/fall and God in His justice, grace, wisdom, and compassion assigned each party their sentence as it related not just to the crime but the intent.

Before I even dive into these details, I need every husband and every wife to know that first and foremost: dishonoring, violating and/or breaking your marriage covenant is serious to God. Above the pain and dishonor you place on your spouse and family; you place that pain and dishonor upon God. You need to understand three very important things when this happens. First you need to understand that ALL guilty parties involved will be sentenced. Secondly please know that NO ONE escapes God's judgement and sentencing. Thirdly you need to know that "true repentance" is the only pathway to leniency.

The first party God deals with is the most guilty. He immediately curses the serpent by making him lower than all other beasts. The serpent must now crawl on his belly and eat of the dust for the rest of his days. He then creates a lifelong beef between the serpent and the woman and declares that her seed and his seed also will be at war.

God moves on to the next guilty party, which is the woman. He tells her that He is going to GREATLY multiply both her sorrow and conception (more pain than intended and more kids than expected). He clarifies by telling her that she's going to bring forth children in sorrow and her despite the pain she's still going to desire her husband (therefore making more babies to continue the childbearing process). The last part of her sentencing is that her husband will rule over her. My God, I felt this one. This gave me so much insight and revelation. If God always meant for the husband to be the head of the wife, why was it introduced here as a curse for Eve's choice/mistake in the garden? Based on all the scriptures presented specifically within this book, I believe it was because God made man with dominion true, but He created Eve to be his help which would have given them equal authority. They existed in perfect harmony together and with God. They were truly "One Flesh", but because she abused that equal authority and broke their united covenant with God, things would now need to change.

The last party to receive their sentencing is Adam. I almost totally overlooked a very important detail regarding the sentencing for all guilty parties in the garden until my mind lingered on the beginning of verse 17 when he said unto Adam, "because thou hast hearkened unto the voice of thy wife..." it was here that I observed the fact that God told them all exactly what they had done wrong that required punishment in the first place. God is not just a God that punishes you for failing. He's a God that desires for you to learn and grow from your mistakes and bad choices. Punishment is to teach us that our actions carry consequences. Our desire to not repeat punishment gives us the incentive to do what we must to not repeat the behavior.

As a parent I taught my kids at a young age to watch for dangerous things like the stove being hot and explaining that putting objects into the wall outlets can harm or even kill them they all listened and never put their hands on the stove but one of my children by God's grace and mercy was rescued as he was about to put a fork in the wall outlet. The loudness of the yell I gave as a panicked mother scared him and dropped the fork and began to cry because I had scared him so badly. I tell this story as an example to us that God is always there warning us in one way or another before we make a mistake warning us not to do it. When we heed to God's warning, we have another opportunity to make things right before it gets too far outside of God's protection/will. However, when we don't listen and move forward in our disobedience and rebellion, we now have placed ourselves in position to receive the judgement/correction of God which can prove to be painful and is often difficult to get back on track.

Adam's punishment was not because he listened to his wife. It was because he listened to her voice above God's. He knew what God had instructed; therefore, he knew it was wrong to eat and so for his part he too had to be punished. Adam's disobedience caused him "paradise"! Adam had an easy life. His home, food, and even companionship was provided for him with no work needing to be done by him to produce it. The garden was made to house him in luxury and beauty. The trees were made to feed him daily. His job was to operate in dominion and authority in managing the earth and the creature within it. He was able to spend intimate time with God daily getting to know more about him and basking in the presence of His glory and splendor, but now his punishment would be hard labor. He would now have to till the ground: planting, growing, and harvesting their food. He would now work so hard that he would sweat at his effort. The second part of his sentencing was that instead of living forever, mankind would now return to the dust from where he came.

8. Life Outside the Garden

Genesis 3:23-24 "*Therefore the* L*ORD God sent him forth from the garden of Eden, to till the ground from whence he was taken. So, he drove out the man; and he placed at the east of the garden of Eden Cherubims, and a flaming sword which turned every way, to keep the way of the tree of life.*"

When a husband or wife chooses to live a life outside of God's will they initially don't believe there will be much difference. But violating God's covenant brings a whole new dynamic that you must learn to navigate through. Life outside of the garden is never quite as good as it was when you were living under God's favor, protection, and provision.

Adam & Eve's sin disqualified them from living in the paradise that was meant just for them. They could no longer be trusted to govern the work of God. They also had been cursed with death and because the Tree of Life was in the garden, they couldn't be trusted with the temptation to attempt to live forever. The amazing thing about God is that even though he passed judgement on them he still gifted them with things they would need to survive outside the garden. God made them coats of skin to clothe them before exiling them.

When he put them out of the garden, he put angels at the entrance with flaming swords to guard it so that they would not ever be able to return. The most important and symbolic thing about this is, their children and no one else who would ever live after their exile would ever be permitted into the garden again. This means that they're exile affected their bloodline descendants as well as all of mankind. Although Adam and Ever where directly responsible for the sin, we all were denied access.

Denied access is exactly the punishment that spouses pass down to their sons and daughters when they chose a life outside of God's will. As I stated in a previous chapter, some spouses feel justified to mistreat their spouse, to leave or cheat. He/she believes that they've found someone better suited for them in that other woman or man. Some believe that leaving their spouse will finally free them to find someone better than the spouse they had. When spouses go through the bad times in marriage its easy to feel like they're not getting what they truly deserve or that them staying committed to their ungrateful spouse is blocking them from receiving the real person meant for their life. These are all lies from the enemy.

People seldomly want to hear the truth of marriage because we live in a society that prioritizes "self" above everything. Everything we see in our culture glorifies cutting people out of your life if they don't have it together or are taking too long to get it together. Our society tells you that if you've grown apart it's better to let each other go so that you can be happy with someone else because the marriage has run its course. My personal favorite is, "your season to be together was up, God is ready to bring what you really deserve, and your spouse was in the way" I'm shaking my head and giggling a little, but my heart feels sad even repeating this foolishness.

The truth is that marriages aren't staying together because people aren't taking the covenant they made and the vows they said to God and their spouse serious. Marriages are failing because people are weak, lazy, and selfish. Marriages aren't lasting because people behave in a dishonest and dishonorable manner by refusing to keep to their word and by allowing a few bad moments in time or mistakes influence a lifelong commitment you swore to uphold. Too many people are running to God's altar to make false promises to someone who's faithful to the promise they're making to their love and their God.

PWhen the man isn't in his garden, his life is full of lack and unfruitfulness. The wife and family will suffer until she eventually comes to a place with GOD where she refuses to live her life outside of the garden. A good wife will surrender her life completely to God in efforts to provoke God to protect and save her children, herself, and her husband. Yes, God does indeed hear the prayers of a wife crying out for God to wake her husband up.

She understands that someone in her home must be obedient to the instructions of the Lord. When a Marriage's conditions aren't favorable to God's plan and purpose, it will experience defeat and lack. It will not just affect the marriage, but it will also affect the children's lives. This is why it's so Important for wives to stay awake. You cannot allow the sins of your husband to lead you down the road of unrighteousness. I have seen the destruction of so many wives as a result of following their sleeping husband. I have also watched the consequences wives face from following a man that's taking his instructions from the enemy.

If a man isn't following God he's being led by the voice of the enemy and it's a horrible situation in the home when you both have been kicked out just like Adam and Eve. Adam knew his wife choice was bad, yet he still chose to eat of the tree when God gave him the instructions personally not to. Adam was so in love with his wife and respected the covenant that he had with her so much that he ate with her and as a result made things bad for so many generations to come.

We were born in sin because of their decisions and so today within many homes we can still find the evidence of the garden when wives are allowing themselves to be led astray by unsubmitted/disobedient to God husbands and likewise when men are refusing to rise into their God ordained authority thereby allowing their homes to be turned upside down because their wife is forced to lead. This is the root of the dysfunction within the home/family/and marriage.

Today God is ready to heal the homes by healing and delivering the spouses. He's requiring and pushing the husband to get back in order, while admonishing the wife to not be reluctant to give it back when he does. He's allowing showing His people the way back into the garden he designed for them and he's restoring families back into right position where they can be blessed and live in abundance.

PRAYER FOR THE WIVES

For the wives that have been in their garden with God planting, sowing, and waiting on her husband to awake from his sleep in order to assist with the assignment God has laid before you. In hopes that you will be able to live in joy, prosperity, love, kindness, and gentleness within your covenant and your family. For the wives that have been standing in the gap on behalf of their husband, the wife that's been waiting for things to turn around for the better, father we ask that you bring their hearts desires into fruition. Their desire for their husband to be the head, to lead their family in the way you intended for him to lead. We come against every enemy and adversary both spiritual and fleshly.

We pray that you close every gateway that has been opened within the marriage and family. Lord stay the hand of the enemy. Raise up a standard against the devil and defend their marriage. Lord give this wife a spirit of humility, patience, love, wisdom, and strength. Let her hope always remain in you. Give her the wisdom to know how to fight against every enemy of her marriage and family. Bless her, lead her, heal her from secret pains and traumas and let her be the best wife, mother, and woman she can be. Father, we ask that you restore whatever has been stolen from their lives so that they may live their marriage life, in your divine will.

In Jesus Name. Amen, Amen.

PRAYER FOR THE DIVORCED WIFE

Father God, I thank and praise you today for every divorced wife all across this world. I pray that you would first forgive us all of our sins and short comings. Lord, help us to become better each day through your wisdom, instruction, strength, and mercy. I pray for every woman who has suffered the tragedy of divorce. Keep this wife from feelings of failure, depression, worthlessness, and hopelessness. Let this wife know that there is still much value within her and that you are not finished with her story yet.

Lord whatever part she played in the divorce heal, deliver, and grant her wisdom for the next part of her journey. Restore her confidence and reaffirm her worth as a woman and wife. Allow her to know that even beyond divorce you are still on her side. God, if there were any injustices, offenses, and abuses committed against her by her spouse we pray that you would bring swift justice. Vindicate her from all lies and scandals that wounded her. Heal every part of her life and fortify her in your strength, wisdom, honor, and integrity.

Allow your daughter to take this time of singleness to remember her beauty, her power, her worth, and her purpose. Give her the mind to submit herself to you by spending time with you daily so that you can be everything she needs you to be. Allow her to wait patiently as you bring either full restoration of her marriage or the blessing of the husband you chose for her. Allow her to be healed, whole, and prepared enough to receive what you have purposed for her. Bring her financial, emotional, health, and spiritual wealth. Let her children be blessed in spite of the things they have seen and heard. Take care of everything that concerns her and bring her into her place of newness in you. Lead and guide her every step so that she pleases you even in her broken season.

Let her take the time needed to heal fully and not yearn for the arms of another man. Have your perfect and divine will in her life and keep her uplifted and focused. Allow her transition to be swift and bring her double restitution for all that she has had to endure. Let her know that you are God and that you will never leave nor forsake her, and that you will be with her all the days of her life. In Jesus' matchless and powerful name.

PRAYER FOR THE PREPARED WIVES

Lord thank you for this single woman who has prepared herself to be a good and godly wife. I ask that you allow her to exist in a place of divine peace, joy of life, and fulfillment within her relationship with you, understanding that singleness is not loneliness. Let her embrace her freedom to know herself, understand your mysteries, and experience life uninhibited while also learning to balance her needs, wants, and desires with the assignments and callings you have purposed for her life.

Lord let this prepared wife continue to live her life honorably and virtuously within the power of your Holy Spirit. Let her be quick and earnest in her repentance and diligent and consistent in her pursuit of you daily. Allow this woman to know love of self so that she may be able to recognize and accept the love of a man. Give her great discernment to recognize when things, people, and even opportunities are not good for her life.

Let her never lack nor enter a place of self-doubt or desperation. Keep her mind and spirit alert and allow her to walk daily within your wisdom, seeking you always for instruction. Heal every pain and trauma of her past so that it may not hinder the blessings of her today and tomorrow. Allow her to learn and mature beyond past failures and bad judgements. Let her be an amazing mother to her children and/or to the children you will allow to come from her womb in the future.

Allow this prepared wife to always find love, satisfaction, and purpose within you. Let her humble herself under your almighty hand. Show her the path to walk in her life that is both customized for her and for this current season of her life. Let her never be ashamed. Bring her husband to her in the season you have ordained and let him be everything you designed a husband to be protective, a provider, a teacher/leader, a husband who loves her with real undying love, a husband that regards her as his equal and his teammate. A husband who understand his role and reverences, respects, and values the role she is designed to play in his life as well. Quiet every voice of the enemy that tries to discourage, distract, or taunt her for her values and desire to please you. Reward her for her diligence and faithfulness to you. In Jesus' Name we pray. Amen and it is so!

ABOUT THE AUTHORS

Patrice Finley is the wife of Maurice Finley and the mother of nine beautiful children: Maurice Jr., Makaila, Miguel, Mauriana, Emmette, Eamon, Eli, Elasha, and Emoni. Patrice is an ordained Minister as well as an affirmed Prophetess of God. She is a woman full of power, grace, and integrity. Patrice is a woman that has learned to balance her many different roles eloquently and effectively. She's a businesswoman who currently owns and operates Kingdom Kitchen as well as Kingdom Construction alongside her husband.

Patrice's love and dedication goes beyond her home and the four walls of the church building as she feeds the homeless and spends different communities preaching the gospel and coaching other women in marriage, life, and ministry matters. Her personal mission and vision for her role as a P.31 founder is to take wives to another level as God allows.

ABOUT THE AUTHORS

Jackie Johnson is an Ohio native who for the last four years has been a resident of East Los Angeles, CA. She is the proud mother of three amazing, anointed, and talented young adults (Mikel, Mi'Kayla, and Mikah Kindell) who have followed in the footsteps of their mother and are all themselves entrepreneurs. She is an ordained Elder as well as an affirmed Apostle of the Lord and serves under the leadership of Apostle/Dr. Dorvetta Price and the True Prophetic Utterance Ministries. She is a spiritual leader, a mentor, a published author of over nine titles, a publisher, licensed life insurance agent, business consultant & coach, song writer, and singer.

Ms. Johnson's educational background is in the Business and Finance arena. She is a woman of honor, integrity, and great virtue. She's a woman who's known love, loss, marriage, as well as divorce. She has not only survived through her pain and trauma, but she came through her storms with victory and amazing resolve. Her life experiences coupled with her education and anointing make her a powerful coach and mentor especially to other women striving to elevate their lives through God's divine power of healing and the strength, peace, and self-determination that comes from depending on God. All of which has earned her the title of "The Boss Mentor".

She has impacted so many different platforms from the religious sector, black and brown communities, youth, to theater & music. She has become a powerful advocate for healthy families and relationships. And she continues this work through her partnerships such as My Sistah & Me LLC, which is home to the podcast and YouTube broadcast, "Sister Conversations in Black" and P.31 Wives Club, which is the home of podcast and YouTube broadcast, "Wife Talks". Ms. Johnson reminds those she encounters daily that no one is perfect, but a good man or woman will always correct their wrongs, apologize for their mistakes, as well as learn from their failures, ultimately rising to the greatness they were always destined to achieve.

KEEP UP WITH US

FACEBOOK:

www.facebook.com/p.31wivesclub

INSTAGRAM:

www.instagram.com/p31.wivesclub

YOUTUBE:

P.31 Wives Club - YouTube

www.p31wivesclub.com

P.31 Wives Club
JOIN US
ON YOUTUBE
BI-WEEKLY
NEW EPISODES EVERY 1ST &
3RD FRIDAY
@p.31wivesclub

WIFE TALKS
Podcast
Every Other Friday
WWW.P.31WIVESCLUB.COM

Made in the USA
Middletown, DE
11 September 2022

72914704R00055